I AM AN OVERCOMER AND SO ARE YOU!!

Copyright © 2018 by Inspired To Overcome, LLC.

ISBN Number: 978-0-578-41902-2

Published by LaDonya M. Pitre

To my Creator, the Omnipotent One, the One whose very hands have fashioned me, molded me and shaped me into who I am. I have never experienced a love as amazing, wonderful, all powerful and perfect as yours. There is none that can compare to You. You are the most amazing Father. You are my Faithful Best Friend, my Confidant, my Healer, my Deliverer, my Redeemer, my Rock, my Refuge, my Everything. You have made me whole. I owe you my life and even that, Lord can never repay you for all that you have done for me. You, Lord Jesus are the absolute best thing that has ever happened to me. I love you with ALL that I am and with everything that is within me. Thank you precious Lord for ALL that you have done for me. It is my prayer that I will walk faithfully with you all of the days of my life. Please keep me Heavenly Father until the end.

To my amazing, loving parents who have made countless sacrifices for me throughout my lifetime, your love has lifted me when I needed it most, Thank You. I love you more than I will ever be able to articulate in words. You mean so much to me. To my siblings and to those most precious family members and friends who made the time (in spite of your busy schedules) to be there for me during my time of need, your love has strengthened me and given me the power to arise from the ashes. There were those who came by to visit, those who picked up the phone to check in on me, those who sent cards, those who sent text messages, those who wrote the most eloquent poems and those who continuously prayed for me. None of your acts of kindness and love has gone unnoticed. I love you ALL very much. I am truly blessed because there are far too many of you to name. I know that you know who you are but most importantly, God knows who you are. May He forever reward you for your gracious kindness, your outpouring of love and your continual support for me. You all have taught me the power of God's love at work in the hearts of mankind. It is the power to heal a broken heart, the power to heal a wounded soul, the power to restore a broken and fractured life. Because of the Christ in you, I was loved past my pain. You taught me that truly, there is nothing greater than God's amazing love {~1 Corinthians 13:13~}. Today, I declare that with one faithful step at a time, I shall move forward. I am forever grateful for each and every one of you. Again, thank you for being the hands and feet of my most precious Savior and Lord, Jesus Christ, the Lord of all. May God forever keep and bless each one of you, His faithful ones. I love you all.

<u>ABOUT THE BOOK</u>

This book is divinely inspired to reach those who feel as though they are facing some of the most insurmountable difficulties. It is designed to bring daily encouragement and empowerment during some of life's most difficult storms. I AM AN OVERCOMER AND SO ARE YOU contains nuggets of inspiration, wisdom and encouragement for forty days. I am a firm believer that with faith alive in you, you can overcome. When your faith is working for you, in spite of life's adversities, you have the power to bounce back!!! I pray that you are empowered to stretch your faith and reach beyond every limitation that has been placed on your life. Remember, You are an Overcomer! Walk in Faith and Behold Nothing Shall Be Impossible for You!!!!

"You Are A Gift"

God delights in you! You are a gift, a priceless gem. God fashioned the most intricate parts of your being. He is the maker of your mind, the designer of the texture of your hair, the color of your eyes and even the warmth of your smile. When a potter molds clay, that potter's hands and mind work synergistically to create a masterpiece. Beloved, just like clay in a potter's hand is molded by the intimate touch of that potter, you have been fashioned and formed by the very fingerprints of God! You are a display of God's mind, of His brilliance, creativity and ingenuity!! When He made you, He wanted to display a masterpiece uniquely designed and sent from Heaven!! Don't despise your full figured hips, your lips, your thighs, your broad nose or even your skin tone. Everything that God made is beautiful. **YOU ARE ABSOLUTELY BEAUTIFUL!!!** When the Creator made you, He declared to the world that YOU, My Precious Child, "Are fearfully and wondrously made" Psalm 139:14; the apple of My eye. Never neglect the gift of God inside of you. Remember your life is a gift. Live it to the fullest and know that someone somewhere is waiting for the release of the *true* magnificence that God has placed inside of you to unfold!! Today is your day—Release the gift inside of you! Start the year anew and celebrate what God is going to do through you! Arise and Shine Overcomer!!!!

<u>Journal your thoughts.</u>

Today I choose to overcome

by:____

____

____

____

____

____

____

____

____

____

____

____

____

____

"Dance"

Dance!!! Every day is a story. Ask yourself today, what am I writing? Will you dance the day away or will you walk around in somber mode, waiting for something to change? Channel your mind in the direction that you want your life to go in. If you want to live victoriously, destroy self-defeating thoughts. Everything about you is unique! There will never be another wonder quite like you. The sound of your soul as you break forth with laughter, the stride in your step, the pep in your pace, your personality, and your style are all things about you, that set you apart. These are some of the reasons why you are so deeply loved. It's also the reason why every day you should enjoy your life--- Dance!! Just like King David!!! Dance to the tune in your heart that stirs up life, joy, peace and prosperity. Create your own music--your life is a song. So dance to the melody in your heart, dance to the beat of the drum in your soul, LIVE!!!! Live a life filled with everlasting joy and peace. Share the beauty of your joyful spirit with the world.

<u>Journal your thoughts.</u>

Today I choose to overcome

by:____

____

"Don't Quit"

Never Give Up. There is power in persistence. Sometimes life can throw obstacles and challenges our way that are just not fair. I've learned however, that regardless of the storm, if the last tidal wave did not destroy you, then you can bounce back. There is overcoming power inside of you. Not only do you have the power to bounce back, but you can become much stronger, wiser and better than you were before. So embrace the disappointments in life as an opportunity for growth that will position you for greater divine appointments. Endure the trials and the tribulations. Simply, Believe God. Believe Him when He says that though you may be tested and tried in the fire, you are coming out GOLD!! My grandmother's life demonstrated the power of persevering prayer. She rose from the cotton fields to produce seed that would become the next generation of doctors, lawyers, professors, and more. She had a resilient spirit that refused to give up, regardless as to how difficult the circumstances were. She possessed a faith that refused to die—an unsinkable, unshakeable faith. I encourage you today, whatever your storm is, simply refuse to give up!! Walk in an unsinkable, undying faith!!!

<u>Journal your thoughts.</u>

Today I choose to overcome

by:____

"Get Back Up"

Beloved, you may feel as though life has just dealt you the worse deck of cards ever. Perhaps you are sulking under the weight of the aftermath of life's latest hurricane. Perhaps the torrential winds of life have knocked you off of your feet. Beloved, take note---the storms of life that came to destroy you were unsuccessful. You don't have to sulk any longer. You can arise from that broken place and live life! As I wrote this, I found myself feeling miserably defeated as I reflected on all the storms that have passed over my life. I felt completely robbed of the joy that I once possessed. The more I began to meditate on what I've been through, my emotions were all bottled up waiting to explode, just like a volcanic eruption. It seemed as though nothing completely aligned with what I wanted or envisioned for my life. Beloved, you too may be wrestling with feelings of anger and brokenness. Don't reflect on the past another moment longer. You can get up from whatever has knocked you down. You don't have to live your life angry over the injustices that you have faced. You can arise and you can overcome! Beloved, take heart and put on faith. What came to destroy you is only building up a powerful testimony for you. God has the final say so in your life. You are a champion. You are more than a conqueror! You are destined to do great things! Regardless as to what has left your life in a million and one broken pieces, there is hope for you! You don't have to stay down! Get back up!

Fight the fight of faith in your mind!! You are not defeated, you are a winner!!

Arise Beloved and live the life!!!

~You've only got one life to live. Don't live it stuck in the past. Live your life

today~

<u>Journal your thoughts.</u>

Today I choose to overcome

by:____

____

____

____

____

____

____

____

____

____

____

<u>**Day 5**</u>

"Be of Good Cheer"

The Joy of the Lord truly is your strength. (Nehemiah 8:10). There is something inexplicable about walking in the Joy of the Lord. Take a moment before you begin the start of the day and just Praise God. Can you imagine what life would be like without Him? Although life has its ups and downs, tribulations, trials, difficulties and hardships, in Him you can overcome. For every trial that you face, remember that you are not alone, God is with you!! He promised in His Word that He would **NEVER** leave you nor forsake you.[1] That is an awesome promise!!! You can live the abundant life, but you must put your faith to work amidst adversity. Our Father came that each of us might have life and have it more abundantly[2]. Things may not be coming together right now, but don't become faint hearted. Rejoice! If you are in a place where your spirit is crushed, know that it is only temporary. Beloved, endure. It is only a test. Let go and Trust God during this momentary affliction.

~In the world ye shall have tribulation: but be of good cheer; I have overcome the world. John 16:33~

---

[1] *Nelson's New King James Version Study Bible*. (Tennessee: Thomas, Nelson Inc.1997), "Hebrews 13:5"
[2] Same as above, "John 10:10"

15

<u>Journal your thoughts.</u>

Today I choose to overcome

by:____

____

____

____

____

____

____

____

____

____

____

____

____

____

____

"Give God Your All"

And whatsoever ye do, do it heartily, as to the Lord and not unto men, knowing that of the Lord ye shall receive the reward of the inheritance: for ye serve the Lord Christ[3]. Make each day count. Success is accomplished through planned effort daily. Value your time by maximizing every minute. God has not given you a spirit of slothfulness. In order to achieve great results, you must put forth a great effort. Whatever you put your hands to, give it your best. Know that your labor in the Lord is not in vain. For your best effort, God can cause supernatural doors to unlock for you! Give God your absolute best today!

~Do you see a man who excels in his work? He will stand before kings; He will not stand before unknown men. Proverbs 22:29~

<u>Journal your thoughts.</u>

Today I choose to overcome

by:____

____

____

____

---

[3] Id. Footnote 1, "Colossians 3:23"

"Stay Focused"

Your God given mission is bigger than the people that are currently in your life. Sometimes we can place such a high priority on the people in our lives to the extent that we become consumed and overwhelmed. Perhaps, we can even get lost in love. God ordained relationships are to maintain a healthy balance and a healthy perspective. We are to love as He loved. Many of the persons who accomplished great feats for the betterment of humanity and not just for their inner circle were people who knew their purpose and operated with a thriving passion to serve others. I'm sure there were often times an inner force raging within them like fire and a drive to press forward and fulfill a God given mission, regardless of the obstacles along the way. Stay focused on the mission God has placed on the inside of you. To whom much is given much is required (Luke 12:48). When God has commissioned you to do great things, sometimes, your inability to stay focused on the task at hand will cause you to stumble. Keep your eyes and your mind channeled into the vision that God has placed inside of YOU!!!! STAY FOCUSED!!!

<u>Journal your thoughts.</u>

Today I choose to overcome

by:____

"Don't Empower Your Haters"

Rejoice in the Lord Always!!! Don't worry about the people in your life who are constantly at odds with you. Take time to praise God for the people in your life who celebrate you and who genuinely treasure and value your life. Don't worry about the people who constantly seek to tear you down, to criticize you, to hold you to your past mistakes and past failures or who mischaracterize and misjudge you. There are some people in life who are like bridges, they help you to cross over to the other side. Appreciate the bridges who help you to cross over. Sometimes they come in rays of inspiration that restore you, and help you to unlock your greatest potential. They believe with and for you that through Christ YOU can achieve the unthinkable!!! Then there are other bridges filled with nails, rough places, cracks, weathered, and worn ground. When traveling across these bridges, you must tread with extreme caution. Nevertheless, Praise God for those bridges too!!! For the people who often criticize you the most help to develop the best that's already inside of you. Make a decision not to empower your haters. Make a decision that no one should have power over your will, mind and emotions. Break the spirit of rejection and empower yourself with the Word of God. God has chosen you and whomever rejects you is most probably, a blessing in disguise!!!

<u>Journal your thoughts.</u>

Today I choose to overcome

by:____

____

____

____

____

____

____

____

____

____

____

____

____

____

"Yes You Can"

Yes You Can: Yes You Will—If Only You Believe!!

Have you ever asked yourself what is stopping me? It seems like there are

shackles on my feet, somehow it seems as though there are chains holding me.

What, if anything, is hindering you from moving forward in power, from arising

from the dung of despair and from reaching your full potential? Have you ever

awakened from a spiritually comatose state only to discover that you were

wearing blinders and that you truly could not see? Beloved, you can live your

best life today. But it starts with you. Life is riddled with unseen tragedies,

setbacks, and disappointments but the power to overcome every storm is within

you. God never promised that we would be free from heartache and pain. He

did say, 'I will give you beauty for ashes[4]'; essentially, a song and the power to

dance in the midst of life's stormy torrential downpours. Now wake up and stop

complaining and feeling sorry for yourself. It will only dig a deeper tunnel of

depression and isolation. Use life's tragedies and setbacks as an opportunity to

triumph. Remember victories are only won after you have been through the

---

[4] *Nelson's New King James Study Version Bible*, (Tennessee: Thomas, Nelson, Inc. 1997), "Isaiah 61:3"

battle. The power to overcome only comes when you have hurdles that you must jump over. So Leap Beloved! Leap!

When I was in high school, right before the basketball game was the jump start, a critical moment to determine who gets the advantage. During this moment, two players meet face to face, half court as the referee tosses the ball mid-air—the player who tips the ball over to his side takes the advantage. There was a popular cheer that the cheerleaders sang as their team player went for the ball. The cheer went a little something like this, "Leap Bobby Leap and get up off your feet, I said LEAP Bobby LEAP!!"

I say to you on this day Beloved to just "Leap Beloved Leap!" Get up and Get out of the Cave of despair, depression and fear! Your best life is only a breath away! Only believe—Yes You Can and Yes You Will Overcome!!

~I can do all things through Christ who strengthens me….Philippians 4:13~

<u>Journal your thoughts.</u>

Today I choose to overcome

by:____

____

____

____

"Breathe"

Now Breathe. No really, before you read one more line just take the time to breathe. Inhale—Now Exhale. I know life can have so many of us running so fast, one obstacle after another, the hurdles of life are seemingly endless. It seems like we jump over one hurdle only to take a few steps and yes, here comes another one. Failure to take time to breathe will often result in collapses, crashes, devastation, and burnout. Remember the only one who should control what you do is YOU! Situations and circumstances, even people only have the power over you that you yield to them. Remember, God knows exactly what you need not only to reach your goal but also to make it to your final destination. So remember to take advantage of the blessings that are given to you by the Holy Spirit. The blessings of peace, favor, and divine grace---a place where you can cast the whole or sum total of ALL (meaning ALL) of your cares upon HIM because He cares for you. Now just as you started on this day--- remind yourself each day to simply Breathe!!!

~Cast your burden on the Lord, And He shall sustain you; He shall never permit the righteous to be moved.

Psalm 55:22~

Ask yourself this question: "Why should I worry when I know that He cares for me?"

<u>Journal your thoughts.</u>

Today I choose to overcome

by:____

____

____

____

____

____

____

____

____

____

____

____

____

"Only Believe"

All things are possible to him that believes.[5] So often, whether consciously or subconsciously we place limitations on our lives. We limit ourselves in our marriages, finances, health, relationships, and even in our vision for the future by saying things like, "that will never happen for me". In life, there can be so many setbacks and disappointments, it is imperative that we stay in faith and continuously renew our minds otherwise we will inadvertently program ourselves to expect the worse while hoping for the best ------what an oxymoron! Have you ever heard anyone say, "Well all you can do is expect the worse and hope for the best"? ___**NEWSFLASH**___---your expectation should line up with what you are ***actually expecting!*** Your experiences will cause you to like a professional bull rider; grab that bull by the horns jump on his back and ride this game called life fearlessly and ferociously. When that bull (life) starts to kicking up higher, (the storms of life keep raging), with your legs up in the air your body being flung from one direction to another (kids going crazy, bills past due, health failing you), you don't know what's next, just hold onto the horns and scream, "I am a Champion!! I'm in it to win it!!!" Hit the bull on the backside, it is not over until it is over. On the other hand, you can become so isolated that

---

[5] Same as above, "Mark 9: 23"

unbeknownst to you, your mind is riddled with negativity, fear, rejection, hopelessness and despair. These toxic mentalities will rob you of your peace, steal your joy and cripple your ability to run the race of life in faith. Your life is based upon your choices. Yes in this life, circumstances, tragedies, trials have befallen most of us. However, even though we can't always control what comes our way we can choose how we will handle it. You can shrink back or bounce back. I don't know about you---But I'm making a choice every day to bounce back—to never live in defeat even self-defeat. I choose to believe God that even when things are at their worse somehow the best of this life is right before me. I believe HIM. Therefore, I know that in Him all things are possible[6]. I exhort you Beloved, choose today—Only believe God, you will experience new life and unlimited visions and dreams will become a reality for you. The choice is yours---Believe Beloved, Only Believe.

<u>Journal your thoughts.</u>

Today I choose to overcome

by:____

____

____

____

---

[6] Id. footnote 1, "Mark 9:23"

"Rejoice"

Rejoice in the Lord always.[7] As I faced some of the most difficult times in my life, I can remember standing by a water fountain and I had three pennies in my wallet. As I dug out those coins, I can remember tossing them into the wishing well and praying that God would hear and answer my prayers. I told God that I wanted to enjoy my life. In the silence, a still small voice whispered, "That is your choice". From that point on, I realized that I had to choose each day to rejoice. I began to ponder and reflect upon all that I have to be grateful for and joy began to bubble up inside of me. I reflected upon those who did not have the activity of their limbs but were still praising God. I realized that sometimes the greatest battle is not in the storms we face on the outside but conquering the storms within. Choose on this day, beloved to Rejoice! Recognize that you can enjoy your life but it is your choice. Choose to rejoice and to be glad in the Lord. Begin to thank God for what you do have and endeavor to keep a spirit of gratitude throughout life. Choose to put on the mind of Christ and war against any other mindset.

---

[7] Id. footnote 1, "Philippians 4:4"

~Rejoice always, pray without ceasing, in everything give thanks for this is the will of God in Christ Jesus for you.

1 Thessalonians 5: 16-18~

<u>Journal your thoughts.</u>

Today I choose to overcome

by:_______________________________________

____

____

____

____

____

____

____

____

____

____

____

"You Have The Victory"

If the victory is in God, of God and from God and HE has given you that same victory…why are you walking around in defeat? Oh precious child of God, why is your soul depressed and heavy within? Shake off that spirit of discouragement, right now! Put on the mind of Christ instantly! You cannot allow the wrong spirit to suppress and oppress you. If given a small window, the enemy will try to slither through the cracks in your soul and wreak havoc upon every area of your life. You can have victory in your life but you must make a firm decision to properly align your mind with thoughts that will bring peace and victorious living. Even if your circumstances seek to weigh you down, you can rise above it. In Christ there is absolutely nothing that you cannot overcome. You must latch hold to the truth of HIS Word. Sometimes, the best thing to do to shake off heaviness and despair is to Praise God until your mind lines up with His Word. Put on your praise music and praise God like King David------- dance until you dance out of your clothes! Praise God until your mind agrees with your praise.

*~Now thanks be to God who **always** leads us in triumph in Christ, and through us diffuses the fragrance of His knowledge in every place….2 Corinthians 2:14~*

Today I choose to overcome

by:____

____

____

____

____

____

____

____

____

____

____

____

____

____

"Move Forward"

Get a New Attitude about life!! Get Up! Get Over It! Get Out!! Life is waiting for you to live it! So spring forth and live your life to the full. Work what **_you_** have and walk towards what you desire. Destiny will unfold, but you my child must take the first step. Will you move forward? Don't look back. Move forward. Take the first step. Just do it, declare on today that "I am walking forward. By faith I am moving forward!!".

~Brethren, I do not count, myself to have apprehended; but one thing I do, forgetting those things which are behind and reaching forward to those things which are ahead, I press toward the goal for the prize of the upward call of God in Christ Jesus. Philippians 3:13-14~

<u>Journal your thoughts.</u>

Today I choose to overcome

by:____

____

____

____

____

____

"Dig Deep"

Success requires a concentrated effort and a disciplined focus. To achieve the unthinkable, to tap into the unmatchable blessings, superior manifold manifestations of God's heavenly treasures on earth, you must keep a keen eye upon God, His plan and His chosen path for your life. Daily you must dig within. There's a reservoir of hidden treasure on the inside of you. But each day you must focus and concentrate. Distractions will come, but keep digging. Discouragement will come, but keep digging. Ants might eat at your feet like a mad hungry dog with a hot steak strapped between his jaws, but keep digging. Snakes will pop out of the ground, but keep digging. Your vision might blur, your body may tire, but keep digging. Everything that you need to make it in this life is inside of you, but you must keep digging. One day as you explore, you will discover gifts, talents, abilities that were lying dormant on the inside of you. Keep digging and pull out the vast treasures that are sleeping inside of you. Dig Beloved! Dig Deep!

<u>Journal your thoughts.</u>

Today I choose to overcome

by:____

____

"Position Yourself"

Fight on dear Christian soldier—Fight on! No man that warreth entangles himself with the affairs of this life; that he may please Him who hath chosen him to be a soldier.[8] Get your mind right. You are on divine assignment. Do not allow the cares of this life nor your present circumstances to choke the Word of God in you. Position yourself for what God is doing through you. Position yourself for the greatest catapult into destiny, promise, hope and fulfillment. Keep your focus on the mission. There are lives that are depending on the ministry that God has placed inside of you. You cannot afford another day of distraction!! You must stay the course. Be steadfast and immovable always abounding in the work of the Lord.[9] Sometimes you may feel like your work is in vain, but trust that your labor in the Lord is not in vain. He sees, He knows and He will reward you. When things get difficult, remember In ALL things, keep on standing!!! Not only will you reach your destiny but God will use you as a mighty instrument to help others reach their destiny too!!!

---

[8] Id. Footnote 1, "2 Timothy 2:4"
[9] Id. Footnote 1, 1 Corinthians 15:58

Today I choose to overcome

by:____

____

____

____

____

____

____

____

____

____

____

____

____

____

"The Power of Perception"

This morning, choose to reflect on the power of perception. Perception is defined as the way you think about or understand someone or something.[10] Your perception of things is your reality. As you focus on your perception of things evaluate the way that you are looking at things. Do you have a healthy perception of that situation? Do you have a healthy perception of yourself? Do you have a healthy perception of life? Do you have a healthy perception of relationships? As I reflected on my perception of myself, I realized that there were some things that needed to change. Much of what I had been focusing on was deeply entrenched in what I had experienced and what those who surrounded me said and thought. These thoughts were bringing my spirit down and something inside of me begin to realize that my thinking was wrong.

Beloved, let me encourage you today to change whatever you may be thinking on that is unhealthy. Who says that a size two is better than a size ten? I was a size two for years, when suddenly I experienced a downward spiral in life and through that process, I tacked on thirty pounds. I had to either choose to see

---

[10] "perception".*Merriam-Webster Online*. Retrieved November 8, 2017 from www.merriam webster.com/dictionary/perception

myself as beautiful regardless of size or be unhealthy in my perception of myself. Your perception is your reality. Although many said that I was beautiful, it was my perception of myself that determined how I ultimately felt.

Taking it a step further, in life I encountered one or two persons who took my kindness for a weakness. These people made me feel like being kind was a sign of being weak. As I prayed and asked the Lord to make me strong, the Spirit said to me "You are already strong". I walked away from my prayer closet like, 'WOW!'. At that moment, I wished I had a tape recorder to record the voice of God so that I could play it back to the one or two persons who thought that I was weak and then I could tell them "Now, take that!". After leaving my prayer closet, I felt so empowered within my spirit. As I began to reflect on the way that I was thinking, I began to realize that I gave too much value to the way that these persons thought. It was my perception of myself that really mattered. If their perception didn't really matter to me, I would not have felt the need to prove myself to them. If their perception of me really didn't matter to me, I would have easily laughed at their comments knowing that their perception was only a shadow of their reality but it wasn't even close to being a glimpse of the truth. Now that I am older and wiser, I recognize that what they think, regardless of who they might be, is not important. What is most important is the perception that I have of myself. Beloved, once you embrace and accept yourself, what the world thinks is of no value. You must learn to see yourself through the eyes of God. You are who God says that you are. If you are overweight, if you have a skin condition, if you have a negative self-concept, it is only what *you* put into your mind that will ultimately determine how you live your life. Beloved, choose to let go of every wrong perception. Take a notepad and a pen and sit down with yourself and with God. Write down every negative thought that you have and bring it to God. He can show you who you really are. If God says that you are a liar then you are a liar. If God says that you are a thief then you are a thief. If God says that you could stand to lose or gain a few pounds, then Beloved it is as God says that it is. You must reprogram your mind to think according to God's divine plan and His divine will for your life. Beloved, you are beautiful! You are destined to do great things in this life! Do not let anyone plant a wrong thought in your mind about yourself. Let people think whatever they want to think while you think on what's lovely and what's true. Beloved, your perception is your reality even if it is not actually real. Evaluate your perceptions today. Change wrong perceptions and you will change your life.

<u>Journal your thoughts.</u>

Today I choose to overcome

by:____

____

____

"Reclaim Your Life"

Reclaim your life. Revival. Reset. Restoration! Rejuvenation! Rejoice! You can reclaim your life, but in order to bounce back, realize that every journey starts with one step. If you have suffered an insurmountable unexpected tragedy, realize that you can bounce back. It begins with one faithful step at a time. Sometimes devastation can be so traumatic that the fear of failure can be a breeding ground for hopelessness, fear, worry and bitterness. You MUST arise in your spirit and decide. I want to live. Decide. I will Live. I speak life! Each day, I will reclaim my life—one faithful step at a time. I am destined for greatness. Therefore, in pursuit of my destiny, I refuse to remain broken, bitter, and defeated. I am arising in my Spirit from this lowly mentality. I make the choice on today to live! I am reclaiming my peace, my joy, my destiny one faithful step at a time. Just as an addict or someone who has suffered physical trauma as a result of an accident must undergo rehabilitation, recognize that you may have to undergo spiritual rehabilitation. You may seemingly appear to your enemies as one who has been knocked completely out. Perhaps your setback is so great that it appears as though you will never make a comeback. Beloved rehab is only temporary. Have a little faith. It might look like you will never walk again but Beloved, God is a Healer. It may look like you will never rise from the shame of wrong choices and poor decisions but Beloved, God is a

Healer. He can heal you from your past and restore your soul. Go through the

process. Even if it takes a while, endure. Before you know it, you will be back in

the race—ready to take your mark, set and go!!

<u>Journal your thoughts.</u>

Today I choose to overcome

by:____

____

____

____

____

____

____

____

____

____

____

____

"Get Rid of Your Idols"

Reprogram your mind. Reshape your focuses. Renew your mind. Be sharp and discerning enough to recognize the forces that zap you of your strength and steal your joy. Stop cleaving to people and cleave to the Word. When you make people your source, you resolve that they are your god. The greatest and quickest way to spiral downward is to become controlled by people. When an inventor creates an invention, there are certain intricate details that are incorporated into that invention in order to make it do what it was designed to do. When God made you, He placed inside of you an ability to know Him and to function on a level that will cause you to be a WOW factor in the earth. You were never designed to merely exist and co-exist. You were created to shine. Each day you must decide to give your mind solely unto God. He never created you to be a puppet for people. He created you for HIS glory. Place the proper priority on people. Don't allow them to be seated on the throne of your heart. When God takes a backseat, Lucifer gets in the driver's seat. When God takes a backseat on the ride of your life, you just opened the door to passengers that will bring destruction and curses.

~Therefore, my Beloved flee from idolatry.

1 Corinthians 10:14~

~Cursed is the man whose heart departs from the Lord. Jeremiah 17:5~

<u>Journal your thoughts.</u>

Today I choose to overcome

by:____

"Challenges"

Challenges. Are you facing any kind of challenge today? Challenge is defined as a call to fight, especially in a duel; anything that claims or commands effort, interest, feeling.[11] Most people will encounter some type of challenge in this life. Challenges can come in the form of sickness, a broken and scarred reputation, broken relationships, conflict, marital discord, the loss of a loved one, betrayal, rejection, abusive relationships, financial upheaval and mental distress, even a lack of self- acceptance. Challenges. The question is not will there be challenges, the more important question is how will you handle your challenges. I encourage you today, to face your challenge. Most people never realize that within the very meaning of challenge is a call, a call to fight. You do not have to be defeated or overwhelmed by your situation. Perhaps, you are dealing with relational issues, family members who all seem to be completely crazy. As you look around at your family, you may find yourself wondering, "where did these people come from?". Don't allow the challenges that may seem overwhelming at this time to zap you of your joy. The joy of the Lord is your strength.[12] Keep your mind positioned in the Word of God. Your family may be acting crazy

---

[11] "challenge". *Merriam-Webster Online*. Retrieved November 8, 2017 from www.merriamwebster.com/dictionary/challenge
[12] Id Footnote 1, "Nehemiah 8:10"

right now, but you stay in God. He has the power to deliver your family and to deliver you too. There is nothing too hard for God. Perhaps you don't have the finances to birth the dream that God has placed in your heart. Trust God, in Him there is no lack. He has the necessary provision to finance what He has given you to do, just walk by faith. Perhaps, you may have sickness and disease in your body, believe God that He is a Healer. Perhaps, life has hit you so hard that you feel like giving up. Don't quit, reposition your mind in God. He is still on the throne. Maybe, you feel like good things will never happen for you, or this marriage is the marriage from hell. Beloved, trust God. Grow in His grace and in His love. Perhaps there are relationships that have kept you in bondage, more depressed than you have ever been in your entire life, a place of utter despair where you are barely holding on to your sanity. Believe God that He can remove the wrong people and bless you with the right people. Perhaps your own dysfunctions and failures have crippled you mentally and hindered your ability to spring forth and shine for fear of another failure. Beloved shake the dust off and Arise Again and Again and Again and Again. Arise! You may even be in a place where the challenges are hitting you so hard that you take that familiar cliché, "when it rains it pours" and use it as the mantra for your life. Change your confession. Child of the Most High God, this too shall pass. Whatever your challenge is, I encourage you Beloved to take a stand, rise up and fight the good fight of faith. Understand that God is with you in the midst of that challenge. He has not changed. His love for you and His promises remain the same. You must change your perspective and face your challenges.

~If you faint in the day of adversity, your strength is small. Proverbs 24:10~

<u>Journal your thoughts.</u>

Today I choose to overcome

by:____

____

____

____

____

____

____

____

____

____

____

____

"Don't Live In Regret"

Your life is ultimately your responsibility. Have you ever heard people say if I would have known my father perhaps my life would be better? If I had not started a family so young, maybe I could be that doctor or lawyer that I always wanted to be. If only I had gone out and gotten my education, maybe my family would be in a better position financially. Beloved, you can forever live in what you wished you or someone else had done. But let me warn you that regret is only a hindrance keeping you from effectively transforming your life. Some people live in regret and die in regret too. You can focus on your failures, you can focus on who did not do what they were supposed to do in your life. You can focus on what someone else did in attempts to destroy your life. What you focus on is the spring board for your life. Your focus will catapult you into whatever has captivated your mind's attention. If you focus on becoming a boxer, regardless of how many hits you take along the way, eventually you will get there if you don't give up and if it is God's will for you. If you are focused on what has never happened or what did not happen the way that you wanted it to, then you will never spring into anything new because your mind is filled with negativity. You can't continue to expect God's best while feeding your mind negative thoughts about what should have taken place in your life. Your life is your responsibility. Quit comparing where you are in life to where someone else is. Your life is your life. Unchecked regret can cause you to compare your current lot in life to someone else's.

For instance, I know a woman who seemed on the surface to be very happy with her life. As I came to know her, I soon realized that she was very bitter. I could never understand why. She often complained about how she wished that she didn't speak so poorly and she wished she had waited before she had children, she wished she had furthered her education by going back to school. While I began to encourage her and pray for her, I eventually realized that her heart was filled with murderous envy. She began to spread vicious lies and rumors about me and continued to tell people that she just did not like me but she did not know why. When these words were spoken to me by others and confirmed in the Spirit, I prayed even more for her. God revealed to me that her heart was filled with envy and that the spirit of ill will was causing her to attempt to sabatoge my life. Why you ask? Because she was unhappy with her lot, her current station in life. Now do you really think that by hating me she was in some way positioning herself for a better life? Of course not. She was only setting herself up for a life filled with insecurity and unfulfilled promises and dreams. Regret is far more serious than some people can ever realize and if left unchecked for too long, it can poison your soul with envy which will ultimately kill you rather than the person that is the object of your hatred. Choose to come out of your bondage. Your life is your responsibility. It is not too late for you to do what God has called you to do. Lay aside the weight of regret and rise up and

do what God has called **YOU** to do.

<u>Journal your thoughts.</u>

Today I choose to overcome

by:____

____

____

____

____

____

____

____

____

____

____

____

____

"You Can Make It"

You can make it against all odds. Sometimes when we focus on what's not right in our lives, we have the tendency to sulk in self-pity and self-defeat. As I look back over my life, it seems like I was always falling just a little short of winning the victory in certain situations. As I reflected on this, I felt miserably defeated. I wondered, 'Why does life have to be so hard?'. 'Why does it seem like I can't get any good breaks?'. The more I continued with this train of thought, the worse I felt.

I was on facebook today flipping through some pictures of someone that I know who has a skin condition. He lived a very successful life against all odds. I thought about the model with vitiligo, she went on to pursue her dreams against all odds. As I looked at their drive and determination to make it in the face of defeat, I saw them succeed against all odds. Even though it appeared as though life had dealt them an unfair deck of cards, they were successful in spite of their situation. It made me realize that I too can succeed against all odds, if only I just believe. Beloved, I don't know what you may be struggling with but let me encourage you today. You can make it against all odds. Regardless, as to where you are, you can make it. You have to think on the right things. If you think negatively then you will only feel depressed. But if you think positively, you will feel hopeful that tomorrow will bring about change. If you have been feeling sorry for yourself because of your current situation, let me encourage you, change your mind today. Live your life to the full against all odds. Rise up and face your challenges against all odds. Focus on becoming all that God has created you to be against all odds. Regardless as to how life may seem to work against you, know that you've got God's favor on your side. You can make it!! You can take it!! You just have to renew your mind to believe the truth.

~No weapon formed against you shall prosper. Isaiah 54:17~

<u>Journal your thoughts.</u>

Today I choose to overcome

by:____

____

____

____

____

____

____

____

"You Are Destined For Greatness"

Beloved you do not have to settle for anything less than God's best. I know it may sound cliché but the truth is you don't have to be mediocre. You are destined for greatness. In the book of Zechariah 4:10, the scripture declares that you should not despise small beginnings. It is often in your wilderness experiences that your lack of character is being revealed and exposed to you. It is a process of purging and pruning so that the real you can emerge. It is a time of mental development and sometimes excruciating pain. When there is an assignment on your life sometimes things will not work out the way that you expected them to. Don't succumb to depression and slothfulness. Do not yield to the mediocre mentality by giving a half-hearted effort because deep down inside you have lost hope, you have become faint hearted or perhaps you fear failure, another disappointment or rejection. Have no fear. Do not half- way do the job, if you are going to do it, do it well. When people think of you, they should think, "Yes, I know that child of God and **everything** she does, she does it **WELL!!!!**" Slothful is defined as unwilling to work or exert oneself, lazy; idle.[13]

Disappointments, setbacks in life can often bring you into a place of

---

[13] "slothful" *Merriam-Webster Online*. Retrieved on November 8, 2017 from www.merriam-webster.com/dictionary/slothful

despondency where you begin to believe that just surviving and getting by is good enough. But God did not call you to be good enough. He did not call you to settle for living with a good enough mentality. Beloved, you are more than a conqueror!!! You are destined for greatness!! Give God your greatest and your best effort each and every day and watch God release and open heaven's best blessings in and upon your life.

<u>Journal your thoughts.</u>

Today I choose to overcome

by:____

____

____

____

____

____

____

____

____

____

"Run Your Race"

Did you know that God wants you to succeed in every area of your life? He is your biggest cheerleader. You must wake up. Each day wake up and purpose in your heart that you will not drown in self –pity because of people pain or relationships that turned sour. I heard a very powerful preacher say that "sometimes rejection is direction". I've learned over the course of my life that we are creatures of habit. Thus, it is harder to get out of a pit once you have fallen into one. I believe that explains in part why scripture says leave no place for the devil. What happens when you hold unforgiveness in your heart for too long? You invite satan and all of hell's army to attack you in every area of your life. When the spirit of bitterness crops up in your soul, the scripture says that it will defile you.[14] Quit dwelling on past hurts. The enemy keeps rehearsing those memories in your mind so that you can remain the wounded runner on the side of the track. He will never want you to get back on the track and run your race. You can sit on the sidelines of life for years and nurse the same old wounds, year after countless year or you can WAKE UP and FIGHT BACK!!! Fight the good fight of faith. Get back up. Shake off the feelings of shame and guilt and run your race. God gave each of us an assignment in life and told us in His Word

---

[14] Id. Footnote 1, "Hebrews 12:15"

to stay the course. You can choose to sit on the sidelines but I am getting up from this pain and declaring, that I will run my race and I won't stop until I reach the finish line. It is my prayer that when I have finished my journey, like the old folks used to say that I can hear my Maker whisper in my ear, "Well done O good and faithful servant, well done". Child of God, GET UP and run your race!!!

~The race is not to the swift, nor the battle to the strong, nor bread to the wise, nor riches to men of understanding, nor favor to men of skill; but time and chance happen to them all. Ecclesiastes 9:11~

~But the one who endures to the end shall be saved. Matthew 24:13~

<u>Journal your thoughts.</u>

Today I choose to overcome

by:____

____

____

____

____

____

____

"You Are An Assignment From Heaven"

Are you enjoying being depressed? Are you enjoying being stuck in a pit of depression? Do you take pleasure in being rooted in fear and grounded in worry and anxiety? Beloved, you do not have to stay in that place. I know it may seem like you are stuck but believe God through the power of His Spirit that He is more than able to break every grip that the enemy has on your life. Some things are simply put, a matter of decision. You must decide what you will believe. You must decide that you will trust God. You must make a decision that the choice to enjoy your life is your choice. Regardless of where you are in your life, regardless of what has happened in your life or what is happening in your life, you can start enjoying your life today. If you feel stuck in a rut of depression, in shackles to worry and fear, imprisoned by the opinions of others, free yourself through the power of God's Spirit and Come Out!! Arise from depression, cast aside all of your worries, fears and anxieties! It is high time for God to be glorified in and through you. When you start moving forward, when you start believing God, you will see God working out what you thought could never happen. I dare you to choose life over death. I dare you to latch hold to God's unchanging hand and stand up to every devil and declare that I am a child of the Most High God! I am an assignment from heaven and none of the powers of hell have power over me! I am an Overcomer!!!! Beloved, Yes YOU are an

Overcomer!!! Rise up today and walk in your victory. Make the right choice. Choose Joy over depression. Choose love over hate. Choose peace over strife. Choose forgiveness over bitterness. Choose blessings and favor and honor over poverty and lack and disease. Choose Beloved to believe and trust God in ALL things!!! God's absolute best for you is still yet to come!! Go out today and enjoy your life to the fullest!!!

<u>Journal your thoughts.</u>

Today I choose to overcome by:____

____

____

____

____

____

____

____

____

"The Power of Decision"

The serenity prayer is one of the most profound prayers that I have read. Oftentimes, we can be so consumed with things that are simply beyond our control. Constantly obsessing about situations or circumstances that we do not have the power to change will not bring about positive change. It will not cause you to flourish. It will only cause you to shrivel up and die, just like a flower that does not receive the proper nourishment. Some things in life are a matter of decision. In life, there will be different darts and arrows that come to get you off track and to throw you off course. But as long as God has given you the ability to keep moving, then dust yourself off, get up and keep moving forward. The decision to get back up and run your race is your decision. You can continue to wallow in the pig sty of self-pity but it will not help you to heal any faster. In fact it will only prolong your deliverance. Life may have thrown so many different blows at you until you feel a sense of numbness and mental paralysis. Even though you are going from day to day, managing life's daily tasks and responsibilities, you are not truly living your life if there is no true abundant life flowing on the inside of you. Abundant life includes a life filled with peace, joy, love and happiness. Beloved, if you are not experiencing abundant life then you are merely going through life. Ask yourself, "Am I truly living?" Each day you may be moving along the course of your life just like a zombie---a dead person walking. You may have lost your joy, lost your peace and ultimately lost your passion for life. Let me encourage you today that it does not matter where you have been, your losses, your painful experiences, leave your past behind. God has provided beauty for ashes.[15] He can restore the years that you have sown in tears. He can and will heal you, if you believe. You must decide to put away past mistakes and past failures. You must decide that you will arise. Don't overanalyze any situation according to what it looks like nor according to how you feel. Just make the decision today, that setbacks are only opportunities for you to make the greatest comeback of your life. Even if life may have set you so far back that you feel like an infant in a forty year old person's body, God is able to remove the crutches, heal the scars, lift the spirit of heaviness that has weighed you down and break the chains that have placed you in a spiritually comatose state. Just like a dying patient receives an electric shock and in an instant is shocked back into life, God can revive your spirit and zap you back into an even better position than you were in before.

Your setbacks in life do not have to be the final chapter in your life. Close that chapter and get ready to write the next one. Get ready to write the chapter that

---

[15] Id. Footnote 1, "Isaiah 61:3"

will demonstrate God's power to cause everything inside of you that was dead to spring into new life. Put your trust in the Lord and decide today that you will arise from the pain of your past and move forward into God's absolute best for your life. Arise Beloved! Come out of the graveyard! The graveyard is for dead people. Peel off the graveyard clothes of depression, despair, hopelessness, guilt, shame, self-pity and condemnation. Spring forth and walk out an even better, brand new you.

"Behold, the former things have come to pass, And new things I declare; Before they spring forth I tell you of them" Isaiah 42:9

Journal your thoughts.

Today I choose to overcome

by:____

____

____

____

____

____

____

"Graduate In Your Thinking"

Think about what you are thinking about. Sometimes it is our very thoughts that keep us in bondage. You don't have to remain stuck. Even in a difficult situation, you can still be hopeful. You can have joy and you can have peace. I know that sounds rather odd because many people believe that you have to hold on to negative emotions when met with a negative situation. Although this is the human inclination to go with how we feel, you can tell your feelings to take a backseat. Graduate in your thinking. Elevate your thoughts by lifting your mindset. Choose to think differently and you will get different results. Yes, you may be hurting right now but right now is just temporary. I'm not focusing on this pain. I'm focused on making progress. Yes, you may not even understand where you are or how you ended up in this place, but choose to focus on moving forward rather than dwelling on your current lot in life. Your life has not ended. For you, life may just be beginning. Choose to stay on the positive side of living. You are alive for a reason. Choose to live and to enjoy your life. It all starts with how you are thinking. Monitor how you think and watch your life take on a totally new heartbeat. Just like a heart monitor is used to gauge the condition of a person's heart, when you monitor your thought process, you can better assess where you are going in life. If you remain stuck in yesterday's mess, how do you expect to move forward? Every day set your mind on thinking forward and moving forward. I can't control what happened in the past, but I can control what I choose to meditate and think on. I choose to think forward. I'm not yesterday's experiences. I am destined for greatness. I will do great things one day. I have greatness living on the inside of me. Great things are destined to come my way!!

<u>Journal your thoughts.</u>

Today I choose to overcome

by:____

____

____

____

____

____

____

____

____

____

"Don't Let Laziness Steal Your Destiny"

The dictionary defines laziness as dislike of work; unwillingness to work or be active. Lazy is defined as not willing to work or to be active.[16] Laziness will rob you of your dreams and cause you to have misplaced priorities. Laziness will cause you to believe that you can put everything off for another day. There are many people who started great businesses when the odds were stacked against them because they had a mind to work. They put forth a diligent effort each day into building their dreams and accomplishing their goals. Eventually, with hard work and a diligent effort, they were able to see the fruits of their labor.

Laziness can make you put off each assignment for another day. Lazy people are satisfied with mediocrity. Laziness will cause you to become complacent with nothing. Laziness creates a pattern of un-productivity, slothfulness, procrastination, a lackadaisical attitude that always desires but is unwilling to put forth the necessary effort.

Beloved, create your best life, today. **DO NOT BE LAZY!** Give each assignment your best effort! As a novice track runner, I remember running a

---

[16] "lazy".*Merriam-Webster Online.* Retrieved November 8, 2017 from www.merriam-webster.com/dictionary/lazy

relay. When they passed me the baton, I took off like lightning. I eventually did not hear any footsteps behind me so I put the brakes on and kept everything in cruise control. I thought that I could coast on in and pass the baton while in first place to the next runner. Usually, for relay races, if someone was coming to pass you, your teammates or other supporters would yell, "RUN!!!", "Hurry, she is behind you, Run!!! Run, she's gonna catch you!!" And for this particular race, I heard no footsteps, I heard no voices, so I strided on in on cruise control not running as fast as I could because I was already in first place. I did not feel the need to exert extra effort because I was already leading the race. In my mind, this pace is good enough. Before I knew it, just like lightning this girl comes from out of the sky and passes me by!!!

Then suddenly, I hear screams "**RUN!!!!** Hurry, catch her!!" But it was too late, she crept up on me with no warning and passed me by, right before we crossed the finish line. Reflecting on that race, I realized that a mediocre mindset caused me to miss an opportunity. I could have passed the baton while in the first place spot, if I had run my race to the best of my abilities. I chose to give a "good enough" effort and I paid for it in the end. The race was disastrous. Not only was I disappointed but so were my teammates-- the other relay runners who were depending upon my best effort.

That experience taught me that sometimes you don't get a second chance. Therefore in the race of life, you must make each stride count. You can't make up for yesterday's mistakes and failures but you can change the mentality that has caused you to give up, or to be satisfied with second best. I don't know what happened to the people who were supposed to warn me that this person was coming upon me, maybe she was moving so fast that she caught them off guard too, or maybe they fell asleep on the job. That's what laziness will do for you. It will creep up on you and rob you of the benefits and the joy that come with diligent effort, accomplished goals and dreams. You may not have coaches, cheerleaders, onlookers in life to cheer you on and to alert you as to where the booby traps- in life may be **BUT** you have got the Holy Ghost running with you and living within you. You can run your race and come out on top if you refuse to settle for giving an effort that is less than your best. Don't succumb to a "good enough" mentality when God has called you to be nothing less than great! Do not let laziness be as a hungry bear that snatches your destiny from you. Don't let laziness overshadow nor kill the true Herculean champion that is on the inside of you! **YOU,** My King, My Queen have been destined for greatness! Walk In It. Each and Every Day of Your Life, **WALK IN GREATNESS!** Beloved, Diligently Run Your Race!

"I walked by the field of a lazy man, and by the vineyard of the man devoid of understanding; And there it was all overgrown with thorns; Its surface was covered with nettles; Its stone wall was broken down. When I saw it, I considered it well; I looked on it and received instruction: A Little sleep, a little slumber, a little folding of the hands to rest--- so shall your poverty come like a prowler, and Your need like an armed man"
Proverbs 24: 30-34

~Laziness is an assassin to your destiny~

"The desire of the lazy man kills him. For his hands refuse to labor"

Proverbs 21: 25

<u>Journal your thoughts.</u>

Today I choose to overcome

by:____

____

____

____

____

____

____

____

____

____

____

____

"Fight the Fight of Faith"

The difference between success and failure is often a matter of effort. I may not be successful the first time around, but I will be successful each time at giving my best effort. With each mistake you make, you may experience some setback but you are also given an opportunity to learn from your mistakes, to grow and to refine your character. Every successful effort does not always start without failure. It is merely the effort that produced the right results that everyone extends great accolades and praises for, but behind every great triumph there is probably a list of unnoted failed attempts, tragedies, hurdles, broken promises and inner battles. When met with the opportunity to give up----Fight the Fight of Faith. Increase your capacity to fight, fight the fight of faith until you triumph and see your breakthrough. Discipline your spirit to never give up!

~Your success in life is within you. Actively engage your mind. Channel your creative energy and your actions into getting involved in the perfecting process. Fine tune your ability. You are destined for greatness if only you believe. ~

Journal your thoughts.

Today I choose to overcome

by:____

____

"Rise Above The Nonsense"

Remain focused. Focus requires complete concentration. Pray and ask the Holy Spirit to keep you and to assist you as you focus upon what God has assigned for you to do. Refuse to becloud your mind's attention with immaterial and mundane things. Some things in life really do not matter. It really does not matter who rejects you, when you know that you have been accepted by God. It really does not matter who celebrates your victories, when you know that you are victorious regardless of who comes to the victory party. It really does not matter that people may have misunderstood or mischaracterized you. When you know who you are, who others think that you are is immaterial to you. The negativity and strife that comes to discourage you is an opportunity to distract your mind through the spirit of offense. Protect your mind from negative thoughts. Disengage from people who are full of drama and confusion. You can't move past the past with people who are dragging you down. Disconnect from people and mentalities that imprison you by locking you into bitterness, unforgiveness, anger, gossip, strife----a mind that will cause you to behave stupidly. The years of your life will pass you by and nothing will be accomplished because of where you chose to set your mind. Free yourself and march into your destiny with power, with passion, with strength, courage and excellence. Focus Forward. You cannot undo the past. Your past mistakes, failures, the criticisms of others, your present naysayers and haters may be a huge weight upon your shoulders but you must choose to press forward. I don't know who coined the phrase "shake them haters off" but I say to you that you've got to shake off hate and jealousy from others and rise above the noise. Rise above the nonsense. Choose to think forward. Each day tell the enemy of your soul that I am moving forward. I am thinking forward. I am pressing forward. I am marching forward. I will and I shall Go Forward!!! The past has no power over me. I have been set free. The only one that can bind me to my past is me. I choose to leave my past behind and press into all of the many awesome and bountiful blessings that God has promised me. Now, power up and Move Forward! Forward Marching Soldier!

<u>Journal your thoughts.</u>

Today I choose to overcome

by:____

____

____

____

____

____

____

"You Are Royalty"

Take off every label that does not reflect your true nature. Life and people place labels on us all the time. Maybe as a kid, you were deemed a nerd because you excelled in academia. Perhaps, you married someone who called you lazy. Maybe your mom told you that you would never go further than your current environment. Do not allow someone else's negative mindset about you, change how you see yourself. Maybe you come from a family of alcoholics or drug abusers. You may have been called square head, coward, fat and sloppy, or ugly and stupid. You may have even been called a jackass. I encourage you don't wear the jackass label. Take that one and throw it into eternal hellfire. Choose never to remember it again. Do not wear the dunce label. Do not wear the stupid label. Do not wear the coward label. Do not wear the weed head label. Do not wear the crack head label. Do not wear the fluzie suzie label. Do not wear the chump label. Take every wrong label off and burn it! You are a sum total of what YOU think about yourself.

~If you truly understand who you are, men are utterly powerless in their efforts to mentally cripple and handicap you. Critics and haters may be able to discourage you for a season but they can never cripple you for life unless you empower them to do so. Daily empower yourself by believing what God says

about you. Your attitude is a reflection of who you think you are, not necessarily

a reflection of who you really are. Allow God to show you the real you. Embrace

it. Take the wrong labels off and put the right labels on. You are: A Champion,

An Overcomer, Powerful, Liberated, Destined for Greatness, More Than A

Conqueror. Beloved these are the labels that are befitting for you—a King, a

Queen, a part of a royal priest hood, a chosen generation--- set apart for God (1

Peter 2:9-10) ~

<u>Journal your thoughts.</u>

Today I choose to overcome

by:____

____

____

____

____

____

____

____

____

"Let Your Light Shine"

Share yourself with the world today. You are a gift, a treasure to behold. Don't hide the vastness of God's richest treasure. Let God show Himself mighty and strong through you. Let go of your insecurities. You unconsciously minimize the big things that God wants to bring into the earth through you when you focus on your flaws and your shortcomings. Beloved, no one is perfect. Don't allow your fears and insecurities to weigh you down. If you ponder on where you fall short for too long, if you keep thinking that you just don't seem to measure up, then you will find yourself in a depressed state. A depressed state of mind can promote a spiritually comatose lifestyle whereby you are not living but barely existing, alive but unconscious, wanting to move forward but unable to do so. It is a place of spiritual paralysis that can seep into and wreak havoc in every area of your life. If you constantly discredit your giftings and talents while enlarging your flaws, you have engaged in self sabotaging behavior that is holding you back from living your best life. You are in shackles and chains, a prisoner of your own self-defeating thoughts.

Break the Chains today and set your soul free. Change your mind. You are good enough. Let go of the feelings of unworthiness and reclaim your life. When you are in bondage, you are of no use to anyone, not even to yourself.

Choose today that even though you don't have it all together, God lives in you and that is more than enough. Greater is He that is in you than He that is in the world.[17] Let the glow of God's love abiding in you shine boldly and spring forth. Arise! Shine; for thy light is come, and the glory of the Lord is risen upon thee. (Isaiah 60:1). Let HIS love radiate through you like the sun shining down upon a field of beautiful lilies, lighting up the star blue sky…your warmth, your creativity, everything about you is unique. You are one of God's most precious gifts to the world.

<u>Journal your thoughts.</u>

Today I choose to overcome

by:____

____

____

____

____

____

____

____

---

[17] Id. Footnote 1, "1 John 4:4"

"Set Your Mind"

Do not conform any longer to the pattern of this world, but be ye transformed by the renewing of your mind.[18] There are so many different vices and forces that would seek to entice you and lure you into a fantasy, an illusion. Satan is the mastermind of confusion and lies and he works in the realm of imagination. That is why it is imperative that you continuously renew your mind and bring every thought captive to the obedience of Christ. To live the God kind of life, you must have the right mindset. Sometimes setting your mind can be a challenge, but you are not in this battle alone. God has given you a Helper, the Holy Spirit. Ask the Holy Spirit for help. He can and He will empower you to overcome the battle within your mind.

<u>Journal your thoughts.</u>

Today I choose to overcome

by:____

____

____

____

____

---

[18] Id. Footnote 1, "Romans 12:2"

"Put God First"

The steps of a good man are ordered by the Lord and He delighteth in his way.[19]

Perhaps, you feel as though your life is one big maze and that for every turn you make there is just no light at the end of the tunnel. Your steps, my child, are ordered. In the midst of the confusion, inside of you there is a relentless desire to excel and to become successful. However, sometimes in life when we embark upon an endeavor, we are often met with unexpected challenges, disappointments and setbacks. When you have faced one dead end after another, one financial setback after another, you can eventually grow weary and wonder when will these battles cease?! Perhaps your marriage is akin to the most hellacious war zone or maybe you just received an unfavorable diagnosis from the doctor, there is still hope. Even if there is seemingly one obstacle after another, there is light at the end of the tunnel. Just keep moving forward. Let the Word of God direct you and lead you out of the wilderness. The word is a lamp unto my feet, a light unto my path, Psalm 119:105. Beloved, put God first and remember that even though you don't always know the end result--- He does!! So even when it doesn't make sense, keep moving forward. Even when it hurts,

---

[19] Same as above, "Psalm 37:23"

keep moving forward. Trust in Him every step of the way. His plan and His direction for your life is far better than your own.

~There is a way that seems right to a man, but its end is the way of death. Proverbs 14:12. ~

~You in Your mercy have led forth the people whom You have redeemed; you have guided them in Your strength to your holy habitation. (Exodus 15:13)~

<u>Journal your thoughts.</u>

Today I choose to overcome

by:____

____

____

____

____

____

____

____

____

"There Is Greatness Inside of You"

All of the hairs on your head are all numbered.[20] God cares about the smallest details of your life. God knows the hidden potential, the true measure of greatness that exists on the inside of you. God has placed so much power on the inside of you not just for your personal satisfaction, but also, so that you can impact and change the lives around you. You were created by God to change the world by making a difference in the life of someone else. Never doubt the power of God to move through you. YOU are God's chosen vessel. NEVER let anyone deter you from cultivating the greatness that God has placed inside of you. Keep your eyes on Jesus!! Always remember, God's greatest miracles can be performed through you.

~Verily, verily, I say unto you, He that believeth on me, the works that I do shall he do also: and greater works than these shall he do; because I go unto my Father ~ John 14:12~

---

[20] Same as above, "Matthew 10:30"

Today I choose to overcome

by:____

"Your Best Days Are Ahead of You"

Are you in the Body of Christ yet you still feel lost? Are you saved and still not living the victorious life? Perhaps you know the Word of God but you just don't see the manifestation of God's promises in your life. Could it be that you are saved but you have not yet acquired a revelation of the truth in its entirety? Take a moment today and self-reflect. What is your mirror showing you? Have you tapped into the creative power, the hidden treasures that God has so intricately placed on the inside of you? Oh how magnificent and how wonderful it is to be a child of the Most High God!! It is an absolute gift from God to be chosen to reign victorious as a part of His Royalty!! If you are having moments where you feel unfruitful, take the time to pray and to study the Word of God. As you pursue wisdom and revelation, God will increase your revelation, knowledge, and strength. Your best days are ahead of you----**LIVE TODAY** and **PRAISE GOD FOR YOUR TOMORROW!!!!**

~But you are a chosen generation, a royal priesthood, a holy nation, a peculiar people; that you should show forth the praises of Him who hath called you out of darkness into his marvelous light (1 Peter 2:9)~

Today I choose to overcome

by:____

____

____

____

____

____

____

____

____

____

____

____

____

____

____

____

"Walk In The Newness of Life"

Are you still carrying dead things? Death is defined as a power that destroys life.[21] God has invested so much power, so much life on the inside of you. There are wells of living water on the inside of you. You can speak life to someone who may feel as though they are in a desert, a wilderness of some kind. Your ability to pour into the life of someone else can be hindered if you are carrying dead things. Are you carrying something that will destroy the very life that God has given you? Make a decision today to relinquish, to loose and to set yourself free from the stench of death which can come in the form of bitterness, anger, unforgiveness, rejection and low self-esteem. By holding onto someone who has offended you, you are ultimately giving them power over you. Thus, you are chained by your unwillingness to forgive. Further, if you are constantly rejected by those of whom you pursue, it's not the end of the world. Don't live under a cloud of insecurity and self-defeat because of someone's unwillingness to embrace the gift of God inside of you. Their rejection can be a stepping stone into greater liberation for you. There is absolutely no person on this God given green earth who should have that type of power over you----the power to ultimately destroy you. If you are carrying feelings of insecurity, regret, shame,

---

[21] "death" *Merriam-Webster Online*. Retrieved on November 8, 2017 from www.merriam-webster.com/dictionary/death

hopelessness and discouragement----**LET IT GO!!** I challenge you to renew your mind today. Take off the graveyard clothes (old mindsets, old ways of thinking, old attitudes), the things that dwell inside of you that can ultimately destroy you and walk in the newness of life! Get a good Holy Ghost blood bath and allow yourself to be washed in the Water of God's Word.

~But we have this treasure in earthen vessels, that the excellency of the power may be of God and not of us. (2 Corinthians 4:7)~

Journal your thoughts.

Today I choose to overcome

by:____

____

____

____

____

____

____

____

____

"You Are Who God Says You Are"

On this day my dearly beloved brethren, my prayer for you is that God would enlighten your mind and fill you with the knowledge of His will in all wisdom and spiritual understanding.[22] It is so awesome and empowering to receive revelation from the Spirit of God. A limited mindset can hinder you from rising into the fullness that God has in store for you. A limited mentality can cause you to possess and own self-defeating and self-destructive thoughts that will cripple your ability to maximize your potential, ultimately hindering your overall effectiveness. Recognize the true worth that is on the inside of you and don't allow anyone's negative opinions about you mold your thinking about yourself. You are who God says you are. Let God establish you. Seek Him for life-sustaining power. You can do whatever God has purposed you to do. Do not let hardships and difficulties cause you to break down. Get into that secret place of simply loving God, trusting God, and releasing your faith in God. You are created with a mighty purpose. You must fulfill your destiny. You cannot allow yourself to continue on a path of mediocrity, distractions, hindrances, delay, depression, emptiness and wandering. You must choose the path of intense

---

[22] Id. Footnote 1, "Colossians 1:9"

focus that will prepare you to be propelled into your destiny. This is the time for you to spring forth and let the light of God inside of you Shine!!!

"Arise shine: for thy light is come, and the glory of the Lord is risen upon thee."

Isaiah 60:1

<u>Journal your thoughts.</u>

Today I choose to overcome

by:____

____

____

____

____

____

____

____

____

____

"Walk In Your Purpose-Yes, Yes Lord"

My soul says, "Yes, Yes Lord". Today if you will just say Yes Lord to your will and to your way, you will begin the start of a life that your mind cannot fathom. God's plan for your life is so much greater than your plans for yourself. He created you for a specific purpose and it is when you are walking in that purpose that you will find an inner peace that surpasses your understanding. When you are walking in your purpose, even though there will be disappointments, pain, and even adversity, the blessing is that you are within the protection of God. Therefore you can have peace in knowing that He is your hiding place, your shelter from the storm, a place of refuge where you can find safety from the fierce attacks that seek to annihilate and destroy the life of God inside of you. The very situations, the obstacles, the things that seek to weigh us down, harass us or even destroy us can be a powerful force that will create inexplicable momentum to catapult and thrust you into your next dimension. Most times it is in our greatest affliction that we learn to pray most fervently. The more we yield to prayer, the more powerful we are in God. You can have victory and authority over every adversity. Use the authority that God has given to you. After you use your authority, rest in the Lord. Let Go and Let God! Watch HIM make a way for you! My soul says---YES! YES LORD!!!

Today I choose to overcome

by:____

"Guard Your Mind With All Of Your Strength"

As a young girl, I can remember my great aunt preaching to the children in my community all the time, "A mind is a terrible thing to waste". As a child, we all thought she was old and a great source of amusement. However, as Paul said, when I was a child I thought like a child but now that I am older I have put away childish things.[23] Looking back on those years, I eventually realized that those words were filled with wisdom. Reflections upon my past often made me ask the question, "What was I thinking?" or "Where was my mind"? Take the time today to understand the importance and the value of your mind. Monitoring your mind is the most important duty that you can ever have in this life. The book of Proverbs 23:7 says, "As a man thinketh in his heart, so is he". Therefore, what you place into your mind is what you will eventually become. If you think self-sabotaging thoughts, you have the greatest potential to destroy yourself. If you think loving thoughts, thoughts of peace, you will be in peace. Your mind directly influences your emotions, your behavior and your attitude. Beloved if no one else ever told you before, let me be the first ---"Guard Your Mind With ALL of Your Strength and with ALL of Your Might"!!!! For surely, a mind is a terrible thing to waste!!!

---

[23] Id. Footnote 1, "1 Corinthians 13:11"

<u>Journal your thoughts.</u>

Today I choose to overcome

by:____

BIBLIOGRAPHY

Nelson's New King James Version Study Bible. Tennessee: Thomas Nelson, Inc., 1979, 1980, 1982, 1997.

The Merriam-Webster Dictionary. New York: Pocket Books, Publishing Company, 1974.

Advanced Dictionary (The Thorndike-Barnhart Series). Illinois: Scott Foresman and Company, 1993.

http://en.wikipedia.org/wiki/MainPage, Wikipedia The Free Encyclopedia.

http://www.merriamwebster.com